PALATE-TEMPTING PIE

Easy as Pie

FOR BEGINNERS AND EXPERTS

By Benjamin Darling

76 PIE RECIPES *from* AMERICA'S GOLDEN AGE OF BAKING

LAUGHING ELEPHANT · MMX

ISBN13 978-1-59583-376-1

LAUGHING ELEPHANT

LAUGHINGELEPHANT.COM

GOOD New PIES!

INTRODUCTION	4-5
GENERAL TIPS, CRUST & TOPPING RECIPES	6-11
FRUIT PIE RECIPES	12-35
CREAM, CUSTARD & CHOCOLATE PIE RECIPES	36-59
ICE CREAM PIE RECIPES	60-61
TART & TARTLET RECIPES	62-69
UNUSUAL VARIATIONS	70-71
INDEX	72

Good enough for company and **easy enough for every day!**

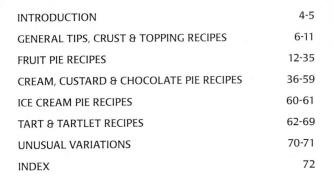

Introduction

The first half of the twentieth century was a golden age for the recipe booklet. Recipe booklets, or pamphlets, most commonly were made by a food manufacturer or kitchen appliance company and were given away as a premium to help cooks learn to use that product to best advantage. Given that the recipes carried the brand, justified the purchase, and, if successful, encouraged repeat use of the product, great effort was made to make the best and tastiest recipes possible. Additionally, after World War II, the quality and freshness of ingredients improved along with the reliability and accuracy of appliances and, most importantly, the housewife (as it was almost exclusively her domain at this time) had more wealth and leisure to cook new and better things.

The recipe pamphlets of this era contain some of the finest pie recipes anywhere. We have included all manner of pie recipes, fruit, nut chocolate and cream fillings, as well as a few pastry and piecrust recipes and tips. Wherever possible we have striven to be faithful to the original recipe, in some cases when it seemed that the recipe was either wrong to begin with, or that tastes had changed to such an extent that most would be disappointed with the result, we have corrected it; we hope you agree.

Pies seem to be especially American dish the expression "as American as apple pie." They are reminiscent of a bygone age when they cooled on the kitchen windowsill and were always in danger of being stolen by hungry boys. Pie is comforting, pie is friendly, whereas cake seems a little standoffish and can be pretentious, pie never puts on airs and is always, sublimely, itself, good old pie. Pie is always better when homemade; the best store bought pie can't compete with even the most mediocre home baker's efforts. Another important consideration when contemplating whether to make a pie or not is that most pies can be eaten for breakfast without fear of censure. Apple pie is naturally America's favorite, and Thanksgiving would be just a big meal if it weren't for pumpkin pie. Pecan pie makes us feel decidedly Southern and cherry pie feels like summer and always makes us wonder if George Washington was hankering for a cherry pie. Banana cream pie seems frivolous and fun, and cream pies in general remind us of people being hit in the face with pies, which is funny because it is the innocuous and lovable pie doing the dirty work, if you hit someone in the face with a different dessert, say a black forest cake or Bananas Foster, it would be a provocative and violent act, and not funny at all. Pies are always circular in shape; if they are in another form they are not a pie, perhaps a tart or a turnover, but not a pie. This is no coincidence; the circle represents unity and wholeness and so does the pie. So enjoy the book, try out some of the great pie recipes, both the familiar and the unusual are contained herein, and recognize that you are making the world a better, more peaceful place every time you eat pie.

About the Author

Benjamin Darling is an author and publisher who, together with his family, manages The Laughing Elephant, a publisher of books and gift products celebrating the ideals and illustrations of the past. He has been collecting recipe booklets for some twenty years, ever since he found a small collection of them at an estate sale and admired the color illustrations of cakes and pies and casseroles.

Notes on Pastry Making

Good pastry is flaky, tender, delicate and evenly browned. It is not crumbly, but when broken, shows layers of flat flakes, piled one above the other with air spaces between.

To achieve this results the cook must be quick and "light-handed" since pastry cannot be good if handled roughly or slowly. The flakiness of pastry is caused by any particles of fat which are surrounded and separated by flour. During baking, each fat particle melts to form a delicate flake. However, rough, slow handling may cause these particles to melt and blend with the flour to form a solid mass, which is tough and hard after baking.

EVERYTHING MUST BE COLD

Chilled ingredients are important for success and for the beginner even the flour may be chilled. A cold, solid fat and ice water are essentials. Mix dry ingredients together, then add cold fat and cut in as quickly as possible. A pastry blender is one of the best utensils to use for this purpose, although a quick job can be done with two knives. [Ed. Note: A food processor is even faster.] Those able to work rapidly enough to work in the fat before it starts to melt from the heat of the fingers may use the fingers. Distribute the fat evenly through the flour, being sure not to neglect the bottom of the bowl. It has been mixed sufficiently when the largest pieces of fat are the size of small peas. These particles roll out and melt into crisp flakes.

HOW MUCH WATER?

The greatest care is required when adding water. No definite amount can be specified since this varies with the dryness of the flour and the amount of shortening used. Usually 2 – 4 tablespoons water are required per 1 cup flour. Sprinkle the water a tablespoon at a time over the flour mixture while tossing it quickly with a fork. Avoid stirring or mixing that would crush fat particles and blend them with the flour. Push moistened portions to one side before adding more water so a dry portion may be sprinkled each time. If allowed to do so the fat-flour mixture will absorb a great deal more water than should be used, so care must be taken to keep the moisture well distributed. Too much moisture makes the crust hard and brittle. Too little makes a crust which cracks at the edges while being rolled; it may crack open while baking and the finished pie will be difficult to serve.

BE SWIFT AND DEFT

When moist enough to hold together under slight pressure, form into a flattened ball (dividing into two if it is a double crust recipe), wrap and chill for at least 30 minutes. When ready to roll sprinkle board and rolling pin lightly with flour. A canvas rolling cloth and stocking for the rolling pin are aids to the rolling out process by preventing sticking without the use of too much flour. Excess flour on the board and pin make the crust hard. Roll quickly but lightly since heavy pressure makes the pastry stick and breaks the surface. Start each stroke at the center of dough and roll to edge, keeping pastry in as circular a shape as possible and keeping edges as thick as the center. Lift and turn pastry occasionally to make sure it is not sticking and rub extra flour over board if necessary. Keep all particles of dough cleaned from uncovered rolling pin since the pastry being rolled will stick to these more readily than to the wood. Roll out to $1/8$ inch thickness for lower curst; roll top crust slightly thinner. Place pastry in pans and bake as directed.

PIE SHELLS

Two Crust: For the bottom crust, divide the dough into two and roll half into a $1/8$-$1/4$ inch thick circle, fold in half or drape over rolling pin and lift carefully into pie pan. Gently fit it into pie plate but do not stretch dough. Trim edges evenly, leaving a 1-inch overhanging border. Fill pie and repeat rolling with remaining half and drape top crust over filled pie. Trim, pinch edges together then flute decoratively with fingers or crimp with a fork. When filling for a two-crust pie is very juicy some precautions are necessary to prevent it from boiling over. The top crust should be slashed to allow steam to escape. One method is to cut the top crust $1/2$ inch larger than necessary and turn the excess under the moistened edge of the bottom crust. When these are firmly pressed together a tight seal is made. Directions for baking given with each recipe should be carefully followed for best results.

One Crust and Baking Blind: Roll the dough into a $1/8$-$1/4$ inch thick circle, fold in half or drape over rolling pin and lift carefully into pie pan. Gently fit it into pie plate but do not stretch dough. Fold the excess pastry under and flute decoratively with fingers or crimp with a fork.

To bake blind – without filling – prick the piecrust with a fork, line pastry shell with parchment or foil and partially fill with rice or beans or pie weights made specifically for this purpose. Be sure to push whichever weights you are using to the sides to keep walls of crust from collapsing. Remove paper and weights after first 10 minutes of baking.

TARTS

Cut pastry into rounds to fit muffin or tart pans, proceed as for pies.

DECORATIONS

Roll out pastry according to directions, and, using extra scraps cut out designs with cookies cutters or freehand. Hearts, stars and crescents are simple to achieve; the more ambitious can attempt Christmas trees, animals, witches or crowns. Place on top of top crust, gluing down with a little water. Alternatively, small cookies cutters or a paring knife may be used to carefully cut out decorative vent holes.

Lattice tops, made with strips of pastry, are another pie decorating method and can be used with any double crust pie.

Basic Pastry Recipes

DIRECTIONS

PLAIN PASTRY

For a 2 crust pie, for a single crust pie halve all quantities

Shortening version

2 cups flour
¾ teaspoon salt
⅔ cup vegetable shortening
4-6 tablespoons of cold water

Butter version

2 cups flour
¾ teaspoon salt (omit if using salted butter)
¾ cup (1½ sticks) unsalted butter
4-6 tablespoons of cold water

Mix dry ingredients together and cut in shortening with a pastry blender or two knives. Add water, using only a small portion at a time until mixture will hold together. Divide into two, wrap and chill. See pages 6-7 for detailed information on handling pastry.

PUFF PASTRY

This versatile pastry can be used in many ways and is readily available frozen.

Patty Shells: Roll thawed pastry lightly to smooth and cut into 3 inch rounds with a floured cutter. Cut out centers from half of rounds with a small cutter; moisten underside of each ring with cold water and place one on each remaining plain round, pressing down lightly. Chill and bake according to package directions.

Puff pastry may also be cut into rectangles and baked for a napoleon-type treat. A tart may be made with a simple disk of puff pastry if the filling is fairly solid, such as apple. For a moister

filling cut puff pastry into square or rectangle and attach moistened 1″ strips of puff pastry to the edges. Chill and bake according to package directions. Turnovers and straws, savory or sweet, are two more of the many uses of puff pastry.

MORE CRUSTS AND TOPPINGS

Crumb Pie Shell

1½ cup crumbs (chocolate cookies, gingersnaps, graham crackers, vanilla wafers, zwieback)
¼ cup sugar
¼ cup (½ stick) butter, melted
½ teaspoon cinnamon (optional)

Mix crumbs and sugar (and cinnamon if using) together, stir in butter. Pour into pie pan and press into place evenly with fingers. Chill for 20 minutes and bake at 350° for 10 minutes. Cool and fill as desired.

MERINGUE (for 1 pie)

Regular Meringue

2 egg whites
4 tablespoons sugar
½ teaspoon vanilla or other flavoring

Brown Sugar Meringue

2 egg whites
¼ cup packed brown sugar
½ teaspoon vanilla or other flavoring

Beat eggs until frothy. Add sugar gradually and continue beating until it is shiny and forms firm peaks adding flavoring at very end. Pile on pie and bake as directed.

WHIPPED CREAM (for 1 pie)

1 cup heavy cream
¼ cup sugar
1 teaspoon vanilla.

Whip cream until slightly thickened. Add sugar and flavorings and continue beating until cream forms peaks. Do not over-beat or cream will curdle into butter. Use as close to serving time as possible.

STREUSEL (for 1 pie) Good on fruit pies!

½ cup packed brown sugar
⅓ cup flour
¼ cup (½ stick) butter, softened
½ teaspoon cinnamon

Mix ingredients together until it resembles crumbs. Place on top of filled pie and bake as directed.

Aunt Jenny's Favorite Recipes, 1940s

Apple Pie & variations

INGREDIENTS

1 recipe pie crust (page 10)
6 large tart apples,
  peeled and sliced thin
1 cup sugar
1 teaspoon cinnamon
½ teaspoon nutmeg
pinch salt
1 teaspoon lemon juice
1 tablespoon butter

DIRECTIONS

Preheat oven to 350°

Line pie plate with bottom crust. Toss all the ingredients except for butter in bowl and put in pie pan. Dot with butter and top with second crust. Bake 40-45 minutes at 350° or when apples feel tender to a skewer.

GRANDPA BRIGGS UP AT THE OLD SOLDIERS' HOME SAYS HE'LL EAT ANY KIND OF PIE YOU GIVE HIM JUST SO LONG AS IT'S APPLE. I GUESS SOME OF YOUR MEN FOLKS FEEL THE SAME SO I'M DEVOTIN' THIS WHOLE PAGE TO **APPLE PIES**

Variation 1

½ cup each brown and white sugar
¼ teaspoon allspice
½ teaspoon cinnamon
pinch salt
1 tablespoon butter

Variation 2

¾ cup maple sugar
½ teaspoon cinnamon
1 tablespoon butter

Aunt Jenny's Favorite Recipes, 1940s

Apple Pie

INGREDIENTS

1 recipe pie crust (page 10)
4 or 5 sour apples
½ teaspoon grated nutmeg
a few gratings of lemon rind
⅓ cup sugar
¼ teaspoon salt
1 teaspoon lemon juice
1 tablespoon butter

DIRECTIONS

Line pie plate with bottom crust. Pare, core and cut apples into eighths; put a row around edge of plate and works towards center until bottom of crust is covered. Pile on remainder. Mix nutmeg, lemon rind, sugar, salt and lemon juice together and sprinkle over apples; dot with butter. Wet edge of upper crust, cover apples and press edges together. Slash top 2-3 times. Bake 40-45 minutes at 350° or when apples feel tender to a skewer.

Jelly Pie

INGREDIENTS

½ recipe pie crust (page 10)
⅓ cup butter
½ cup sugar
3 tablespoons salt
Dash of salt
3 egg yolks
Juice of ½ lemon
¾ cup red currant jelly
3 egg whites
6 tablespoons sugar

DIRECTIONS

Preheat oven to 450°

Cream butter thoroughly, add sugar gradually, and cream together well. Add flour and salt, and beat until light and fluffy. Add egg yolks, beat thoroughly; then add lemon juice and jelly gradually, beating well. Line a deep 9-inch pie plate with pastry, pour in the jelly mixture and bake ten minutes in hot oven (450°.) Decrease heat to moderate (350°.) and continue baking 20 minutes longer. Cover with a meringue made by beating the sugar into the egg whites until stiff. Return to moderate oven (350°) and bake 15 minutes.

Secrets of the Jam Cupboard, 1932

A Short History of the Banana, 1910s

Banana Pie

INGREDIENTS

½ recipe pie crust (page 10)
1 cup of mashed banana
½ cup of sugar
½ cup of milk
½ teaspoon of salt
⅓ teaspoon of cinnamon
1 egg
⅓ cup of cream
Grated rind and juice of ½ lemon

DIRECTIONS

Preheat oven to 350°

Mix the ingredients together and bake until firm in a pie pan lined with pastry. Bake at 350° for 45 minutes or until filling is set.

Strawberry Pie

INGREDIENTS

CRUST AND GLAZE

½ recipe pie crust (page 10)
2 tablespoons sugar
1 tablespoon water

STRAWBERRY SYRUP

½ cup sugar
½ cup chopped strawberries
2 cups boiling water
1 teaspoon cornstarch
1 teaspoon cold water

DIRECTIONS

Preheat oven to 450°

Boil sugar and water and set aside. Line pie pan with crust and bake blind (see pages 6-7) for 10 minutes at 450°. Remove foil and pie weights (or rice or beans), brush crust with crust glaze and return to oven until syrup hardens, 1 to 2 minutes. Cool.

Fill baked crust with fresh strawberries.

Bring sugar, strawberries and water to a boil. Strain well. Stir cold water and cornstarch together, Add to strained mixture. Return to medium heat and stir until thickened. Pour over strawberry pie. Serve either warm or cold.

Aunt Jane's Vintage Pie

INGREDIENTS

1 recipe pie crust (page 10)
1 quart Purple or red grapes,
  halved,
    seeded if necessary
¾ cup sugar
1½ tablespoons lemon juice
  grated rind of 1 orange
1 tablespoon cornstarch
Whipped cream (page 11)

DIRECTIONS

Divide pie crust into two, line pie pan with half. Roll out remaining half and cut into 1″ strips and set aside. Mix grapes, sugar, lemon juice, rind and cornstarch. Pour into prepared pan. With pastry strips form a lattice atop pie, moistening ends and pressing onto edge of bottom crust. Bake at 450° for 10 minutes, lower heat to 350° and bake 20 minutes longer. Cool and serve topped with whipped cream.

19

Advertisement, 1934

Bettina's Best Desserts, 1923

Bettina's Basic Pumpkin Pie

INGREDIENTS

½ recipe pie crust (page 10)
1½ cups steamed mashed
   pumpkin (or canned pumpkin
   may be substituted)
2 eggs
1 cup brown sugar
1 teaspoon ground cinnamon
¼ teaspoon ground cloves
¼ teaspoon ground nutmeg
¼ teaspoon ground ginger
¼ teaspoon allspice
½ teaspoon salt
1½ cups milk

DIRECTIONS

Preheat oven to 350°

Beat the eggs and add all the rest of the ingredients. Beat for two minutes and pour into an unbaked pie shell. Bake at 350° for 45 minutes or until filling is set. Cool and serve.

Lemon Meringue Pie

INGREDIENTS

1 cup sugar
1½ cups boiling water
3 tablespoons cornstarch
3 tablespoons flour
1 teaspoon salt
2 eggs
Grated rind of 1 lemon
½ cup lemon juice

DIRECTIONS

Sift dry ingredients. Add water and cook in double boiler until thick (15 minutes.) Add slightly beaten egg yolks and cook 2 minutes longer. Then add lemon juice and grated rind. Cool and turn into baked pie shell. Cover with meringue made by beating egg whites until frothy – adding 4 tablespoons sugar and ¼ teaspoon baking powder and continue beating until stiff. Put into moderate oven (325°) for 15 minutes to brown.

Cranberry Meringue Pie

INGREDIENTS

½ recipe pie crust baked blind
  or
1 recipe crumb crust (page 10-11)
1¾ cup granulated sugar
¾ cup cold water
4 cups cranberries
2 tablespoons flour
4 eggs, separated
¼ teaspoon salt
2 tablespoons butter
1 teaspoon vanilla extract
4 tablespoons powdered sugar

DIRECTIONS

Preheat oven to 450°

Cook sugar and water to a syrup; add cranberries. Cook until they stop popping; cool a little. Mix flour, salt and yolks of eggs until smooth; stir in 3 tablespoons of the juice of the cooked cranberries; then add to the berries and simmer for 3 minutes. Stir in butter and vanilla; and set aside to cool. Turn filling into prepared crust, cover with meringue made from stiffly beaten whites of eggs and powdered sugar (see page 11). Bake in 450° oven until meringue is set and lightly browned

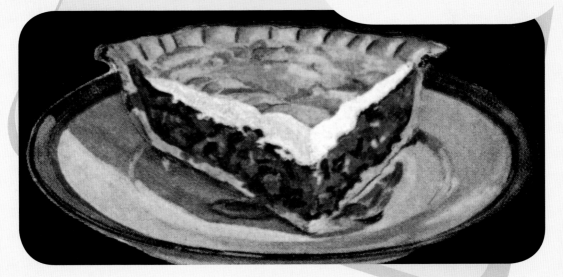

Marvel Lemon Pie

INGREDIENTS

½ recipe pie crust baked blind
 or
1 recipe crumb crust (page 10-11)
1 package lemon Jell-O
¾ cup sugar
¼ teaspoon salt
Grated rind & juice of 2 lemons
1¾ cups boiling water
2 egg yolks
Whipped cream (page 11)

DIRECTIONS

Preheat oven to 450°

Combine Jell-O, sugar, salt, and lemon rind with 3 tablespoon water. Whisk egg yolks in a small bowl and gradually whisk in about ¼ cup of the boiling water to prevent them from curdling. Add to Jell-O with remaining water, stirring until Jell-O is dissolved. Add lemon juice. Chill. When slightly thickened turn into a cold baked pie shell. Chill until firm. Cover with whipped cream.

Orange Blossom Pie

INGREDIENTS

ORANGE PASTRY

1½ cups flour
1 tablespoon sugar
½ teaspoon salt
Grated rind of ½ orange
½ cup shortening
5 tablespoons orange juice

ORANGE FILLING

2 cups milk
½ cup instant tapioca
½ cup sugar
⅛ teaspoon salt
Grated rind of ½ orange
2 eggs, separated
½ cup shredded coconut

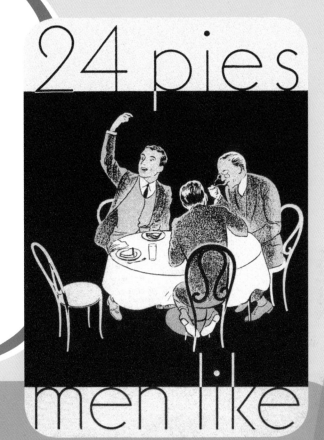

DIRECTIONS

Preheat oven to 400°

Mix all dry ingredients. Add orange rind. Cut in shortening coarsely. Add orange juice (5 tablespoons should bind ingredients together.) Roll out on lightly floured board. Line pie plate very closely with pastry. Prick bottom and sides, line pastry shell with parchment of wax paper and partially fill with rice or beans or pie weights made specifically for this purpose. Be sure to push whichever weights you are using to the sides to keep walls of crust from collapsing. Remove paper and weights after first 10 minutes of baking and bake 5 more minutes. Cool. Leave oven on.

Heat milk in double boiler. Mix tapioca, sugar, and salt. Stir into milk. Cook until mixture begins to thicken. Add orange rind. Cook 15 minutes and stir to prevent lumping. Add beaten egg yolks and cook 1 minute longer. Cool. Then fold in stiffly beaten egg whites. Pour into pastry shell. Sprinkle top with coconut. Bake in 400° until lightly browned. Chill thoroughly.

Golden Lace Peach Pie

INGREDIENTS

1 recipe pie crust (page 10)

3 cups canned sliced peaches, drained

½ cup brown sugar, firmly packed

⅓ cup peach syrup

2 tablespoons lemon juice

2½ tablespoons quick cooking tapioca (or 3½ tablespoons flour or cornstarch)

⅛ teaspoon salt

1 teaspoon grated orange rind

¼ teaspoon almond extract

1 tablespoon butter or margarine

DIRECTIONS

Preheat oven to 425°

Divide pie crust into two, line pie pan with half. Roll out remaining half and cut into ½″ strips and set aside.

Combine remaining ingredients except butter. Fill pie shell with peach mixture. Dot with butter. Lay 7 strips over peaches; lay 7 more strips across them diagonally. Fasten ends of strips to rim. Bake 50-60 minutes.

Pumpkin Pie

INGREDIENTS

1 cup pure, fresh or canned
  pumpkin
½ teaspoon salt
½ teaspoon ginger
½ teaspoon cloves
2 teaspoons cinnamon
3 eggs
1 cup sweetened condensed milk
1 cup water
Unbaked pie crust

Sh-h-h! A secret…
how to make richer, creamier
Pumpkin Pie !

DIRECTIONS

Mix ingredients in the order given; pour into pan lined with unbaked crust. Bake in a hot oven (450°) for about ten minutes, then reduce the temperature to moderate (350°) and bake for about thirty-five additional minutes, or until the filling has set.

27   Advertisement, 1927

PIES MEN LIKE

20 PIES THAT MEN LIKE BEST

FRUIT — BERRY — CREAM — MERINGUE

PLUS

SECRETS OF FLAKY PASTRY

HOW TO GLAZE PASTRY

FOR PERFECT PIE MERINGUE

KEEP THE LOWER CRUST CRISP

BEST APPLES FOR PIES

Pies Men Like, 1953

Cherry Pie

INGREDIENTS

1 recipe pie crust (page 10)
3½ cups pitted,
    fresh sour red cherries
1¼ cups sugar
¼ cup flour
1 tablespoon butter or margarine
Cinnamon

DIRECTIONS

Preheat oven to 400°

Combine cherries, sugar, and flour. Line 9 inch pie pan using half of the pastry. Roll out remaining pastry for top crust and cut several slits for steam to escape. Pour fruit mixture into pie shell. Dot with butter or margarine; sprinkle with cinnamon. Adjust top crust on pie. Seal edges, trim and flute. Or, omit top crust, cut spray of cherries from pastry (see picture, page 28); place on top. Bake 50 to 60 minutes.

Note: Drained frozen or canned cherries may be used in place of fresh. Decrease amount to 3 cups and cut sugar in half.

Pies Men Like, 1953

Blueberry Pie

INGREDIENTS

1 recipe pie crust (page 10),
1 quart fresh blueberries
1 teaspoon vinegar
2 tablespoons butter or margarine
1 cup sugar
2 tablespoons flour
Nutmeg

DIRECTIONS

Wash and pick over blueberries. Line a 9 inch pie pan using half the pastry. Roll out remaining pastry for the top crust. Combine vinegar, sugar, and flour. Add to the blueberries and mix lightly. Pour into pie pan and sprinkle with nutmeg. Dot with butter or margarine. Moisten edge of pastry with water; cover with top crust. Trim; press edges together with tines of a fork. Prick top crust to allow steam to escape. Or cut pastry for top in long strips about ¾″ wide. Arrange over berries in circles, as shown left. Bake in hot oven, 425°, reduce heat to moderately hot, 375°, and bake 25 minutes longer, or until brown.

How to glaze pastry: 1. Before baking, brush top crust with melted butter; sprinkle with sugar. 2. Brush with slightly beaten egg yolk diluted with a little cold water. 3. Brush with slightly beaten egg white; sprinkle with sugar. 4. Brush with heavy cream; sprinkle with sugar.

Pies Men Like, 1953

Strawberry Custard Pie

DIRECTIONS

Preheat oven to 425°

Combine eggs, sugar, and salt. Add milk slowly; stir in vanilla. Pour into pie shell. Bake 40 minutes, or till knife inserted near rim comes out clean. Chill.

Wash strawberries; hull. Simmer 1 cup of the berries, sugar, and 1 cup of the water 15 minutes. Mix remaining water with cornstarch; add to cooked berries. Cook until thick, stirring constantly; cool. Add cooked berries. Spoon over pie. Chill.

INGREDIENTS

½ recipe pie crust (page 10)
3 eggs, slightly beaten
6 tablespoons sugar
¼ teaspoon salt
3 cups milk
1 teaspoon vanilla
1 quart strawberries
1 cup sugar
1⅓ cups water
3 tablespoons cornstarch

Picture Treasury of Good Cooking, 1953

Rhubarb Pie

INGREDIENTS

1 recipe pie crust (page 10)
1 cup sugar
3 tablespoons flour
1 egg beaten
2 cups rhubarb cut into small pieces

DIRECTIONS

Preheat oven to 400°

Line 8″ pie plate with pastry. Sift sugar and flour together and combine with beaten egg. Stir rhubarb into mixture. Pour into pastry lined pie plate. Cover with top crust or lattice crust, trim and seal. Bake about 35 minutes.

33

Praise for the Cook, 1959

Cherry Pie

INGREDIENTS

1 recipe pie crust (page 10)
1 cup sugar
¼ cup flour
3½ cups red sour pitted cherries, drained
¾ cup cherry juice
½ teaspoon almond extract

DIRECTIONS

Preheat oven to 400°

Mix sugar and flour in saucepan. Stir in cherries, juice and flavoring. Cook over medium heat, stirring constantly until mixture thickens and boils. Pour into pastry lined plate. Place top crust over filling, trim and seal. Prick to allow for escape of steam. Bake in hot oven about 30 minutes or until crust is nicely browned.

CHERRY PIE VARIATIONS

Cherry Apple Pie

Use 2 cups sliced apples and 2 cups pitted cherries for 9″ pie. Add 1 teaspoon cinnamon and ½ teaspoon nutmeg with other ingredients. Bake as usual.

Cherry Nut Pie

Add 1 cup slivered almonds or chopped nuts to basic cherry pie filling. Bake as usual.

Cherry Pineapple Pie

Use 1½ cups pineapple chunks and 2 cups cherries. Use only ½ cup sugar. Bake as usual.

Praise for the Cook, 1959

Chocolate Cream Pie

INGREDIENTS

½ recipe pie crust baked blind
  or
1 recipe crumb crust (page 10-11)
1½ cups cold milk
2 ounces baking chocolate
  melted
2 tablespoons flour
3 tablespoons cornstarch
1 cup sugar
½ teaspoon salt
4 egg yolks slightly beaten
2 tablespoons butter
1½ teaspoons vanilla

DIRECTIONS

Preheat oven to 300°

Scald 2 cups milk with melted chocolate in double boiler, beating until smooth. Sift flour, cornstarch, sugar and salt together twice. Mix with remaining ½ cup of milk. Add to chocolate mixture, stirring constantly until thickened. Cook 10 minutes longer. Remove from stove, add beaten egg yolks, and beat thoroughly. Add butter and vanilla. Cool. Pour into baked shell. Cover with meringue made by folding 8 tablespoons sugar into 4 egg whites stiffly beaten. Bake 12 minutes at 300° or until delicate brown.

Angel Chocolate Pie Dessert

INGREDIENTS

12 graham crackers, rolled fine
⅓ cup butter, softened
¾ cup fine sugar, sifted
1 ounce Hershey's Baking
  Chocolate, melted
3 egg yolks, well beaten
1 teaspoon vanilla
3 egg whites beaten stiff

DIRECTIONS

Preheat oven to 300°

Mix rolled crackers with softened butter and 1 tablespoon sugar. Press mixture in smooth layer against bottom and sides of well buttered pie plate to form crust. Melt chocolate in double boiler. Combine beaten yolks with remaining sugar, and add to chocolate. Blend and cook over hot water until thick, stirring frequently. Cool. Add vanilla. Fold in stiff whipped whites. Pour into crust. Bake 30 minutes. Garnish with chilled whip cream. Makes one 7" pie. Note: Cool mixture well before folding in whipped whites, and watch baking carefully.

Butterscotch Pie

INGREDIENTS

½ recipe pie crust baked blind
  or
1 recipe crumb crust (page 10-11)
1½ cups brown sugar
3 tablespoons cornstarch
⅛ teaspoon salt
3 egg yolks
1½ cups milk
1½ tablespoons butter
1 teaspoon vanilla
1 recipe meringue (page 11)

DIRECTIONS

Preheat oven to 350°

Mix sugar, cornstarch and salt. Add beaten egg yolks, milk and butter. Cook in double boiler, stirring until thick. Cool somewhat, add vanilla, and pour into baked pastry shell. Prepare meringue and pile lightly on butterscotch filling. Bake 15 minutes, until meringue browns.

Coconut Cream Pie

INGREDIENTS

½ recipe pie crust baked blind or
1 recipe crumb crust (page 10-11)
⅓ cup flour
½ cup sugar
2 cups milk, scalded
2 egg yolks, well beaten
1 cup shredded coconut
1 teaspoon vanilla
1 recipe meringue (page 11)

DIRECTIONS

Combine flour, sugar, and salt; add milk. Cook in double boiler until thickened, stirring constantly. Pour small amount of mixture over egg yolks, stirring vigorously. Return to double boiler and cook 10 minutes longer. Add coconut and vanilla. Cool and pour into pie shell. Prepare meringue and pile lightly on coconut filling. Bake 12 minutes, or until delicate brown.

New Cake Secrets, 1931

Good Pies
— easy to make

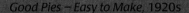

Good Pies – Easy to Make, 1920s

Custard Pie

INGREDIENTS

½ recipe pie crust (page 10)
2 eggs
¼ cup sugar
1½ cups milk
pinch salt
¼ teaspoon nutmeg

DIRECTIONS

Preheat oven to 475°

Beat egg lightly, add sugar and salt. Add milk slowly, beating well. Pour into prepared pie shell , sprinkle with nutmeg and bake at 475° for ten minutes. Reduce heat to 425° and bake until custard is firm and lightly browned.

Good Pies – Easy to Make, 1920s

Molasses Crumb Pie

INGREDIENTS

½ recipe pie crust (page 10)
¾ cup flour
½ cup brown sugar
¼ teaspoon salt
½ teaspoon cinnamon
⅛ teaspoon nutmeg
⅛ teaspoon ginger
⅛ teaspoon cloves
2 tablespoons butter or margarine
½ cup light molasses
1 egg yolk
½ teaspoon baking soda dissolved in ¾ cup boiling water

DIRECTIONS

Preheat oven to 425°

Line pie pan with crust . Combine flour, sugar, salt, and spices. Work in shortening as for pie crust. Blend molasses and egg yolk with hot water and soda. Sprinkle bottom of crust generously with crumbs, add a layer of liquid and continue to alternate the two mixtures until the shell is filled (crumbs should always be on top.) Bake until crust edges are slightly brown, reduce heat to 350° and continue baking until firm (about 20 minutes.) Serve with slightly sweetened whipped cream.

Coronation Butterscotch Pie

INGREDIENTS

1 recipe pie crust (page 10)

FILLING

1¼ cup brown sugar
⅓ cup flour
½ teaspoon salt
2 cups milk, scalded
3 egg yolks
1 tablespoon butter or margarine

MERINGUE

3 egg whites
6 tablespoons sugar

DIRECTIONS

Preheat oven to 425°

Prepare crust and divide into three parts. After chilling roll each part into an 8″ – 9″ circle. Place separately on baking sheets, pricking each well. Bake until delicately brown. Cool.

Lower oven temperature to 325°

Blend sugar, flour and salt together. Add milk and cook until mixture thickens. Just before removing from stove, stir in beaten yolks and shortening. Cool.

Close to serving time put pie together like a layer cake, alternating crust and filling. Prepare meringue: Beat egg whites until frothy, then add sugar, two tablespoons at a time, and continue baking until stiff. Cover pie with meringue. Brown slightly in a 325° oven. Serve as soon as cool.

Chocolate Sundae Pie

INGREDIENTS

½ recipe pie crust baked blind
  or
1 recipe crumb crust (page 10-11)
1 cup evaporated milk
½ cup water
¼ teaspoon nutmeg
3 eggs, separated
½ cup sugar
⅛ teaspoon salt
1 tablespoon gelatine
3 tablespoons cold water
½ teaspoon vanilla
1 cup sweetened whipped cream
4 tablespoons grated chocolate

DIRECTIONS

Heat milk and one-half cup water in double boiler with nutmeg. Beat egg yolks with sugar and salt until light. Pour the hot milk over the egg yolk mixture, return to double boiler and cook until the consistency of thick cream. Remove from fire, add the gelatine which has been soaking five minutes in cold water. Add vanilla. Cool. When cool and ready to set, beat and fold in the stiffly beaten egg whites. Pour into a baked and cooled pie shell. Set in refrigerator. When thoroughly cold, cover with sweetened whipped cream and sprinkle with grated chocolate.

Standard Recipe for Cream Pie

INGREDIENTS

1 cup evaporated milk
1 cup water
¾ cup granulated sugar
¼ cup flour
¼ teaspoon salt
2 eggs, separated
1 tablespoon butter
1 teaspoon flavoring
Baked pie shell (8 inch)

DIRECTIONS

Blend evaporated milk with water. Mix ½ cup sugar, flour and salt. Add enough milk to make a smooth paste. Bring remaining milk to a scalding point in a double boiler. Add flour mixture. Stir constantly until mixture thickens. Cover and cook ten minutes. Pour gradually over well-beaten egg yolks. Return to double boiler and cook until egg is set. Remove from fire. Add butter. Cool. Add flavoring and pour into baked pie shell. Cover top with meringue made by beating egg whites until stiff and adding remaining 1/4 cup sugar. Bake 15 minutes in moderate oven (350°) until brown.

Caramel Pecan Cream Pie

INGREDIENTS

1 cup evaporated milk
1 cup water
¾ cup granulated sugar
¼ cup flour
¼ teaspoon salt
2 eggs, separated
1 tablespoon butter
1 teaspoon flavoring
Baked pie shell (8 inch)

DIRECTIONS

Process as for standard recipe cream pie, using one cup brown sugar in place of granulated sugar and adding an additional tablespoon of butter. When cream mixture is cool, stir in 1/2 cup finely chopped pecan nut meats. Flavor with vanilla and pour into a baked pie shell (8 inch.) Cover with meringue. Sprinkle top of meringue with chopped pecan nut-meats. Bake as directed for cream pie.

Graham Cracker Cream Pie

INGREDIENTS

1 recipe crumb crust (page 10-11)
2 tablespoons cornstarch
¼ cup sugar
¼ teaspoon salt
2 cups scalded milk
3 egg yolks, slightly beaten
1 teaspoon vanilla

DIRECTIONS

Mix thoroughly cornstarch, sugar and salt – add slowly to hot milk. Blend thoroughly. Cook in double boiler 15 minutes, stirring frequently. Blend a little of this mixture with egg yolks, return to double boiler, stir and cook until eggs are set about 2 minutes. Add vanilla, pour into cracker crust.

MERINGUE

Make a meringue of 3 stiffly beaten egg whites and 3 tablespoons granulated sugar. Spread on top custard filling. Sprinkle meringue with remaining crumbs. Bake at 300° until lightly browned – about 20 minutes.

Chocolate Coconut Cream Pie

INGREDIENTS

Famous Chocolate Wafers
2 cups milk
2½ tablespoons cornstarch
½ cup sugar   ¼ teaspoon salt
1 egg   ½ teaspoon vanilla
½ cup whipping cream
1 cup grated fresh coconut

DIRECTIONS Line an 8" pie plate with *Famous Chocolate Wafers,* cutting enough in halves to stand up around inside of plate. Scald milk. Mix cornstarch, sugar and salt thoroughly. Add gradually to hot milk, stirring until thickened. Continue to cook 10 minutes longer stirring occasionally. Pour slowly over egg, blending well and return to double boiler and cook 2 minutes longer. Cool. Pour into chocolate wafer lined pie plate. Spread whipped cream on top and sprinkle with grated coconut.

The Particular Cook's Cook-Book, 1930s

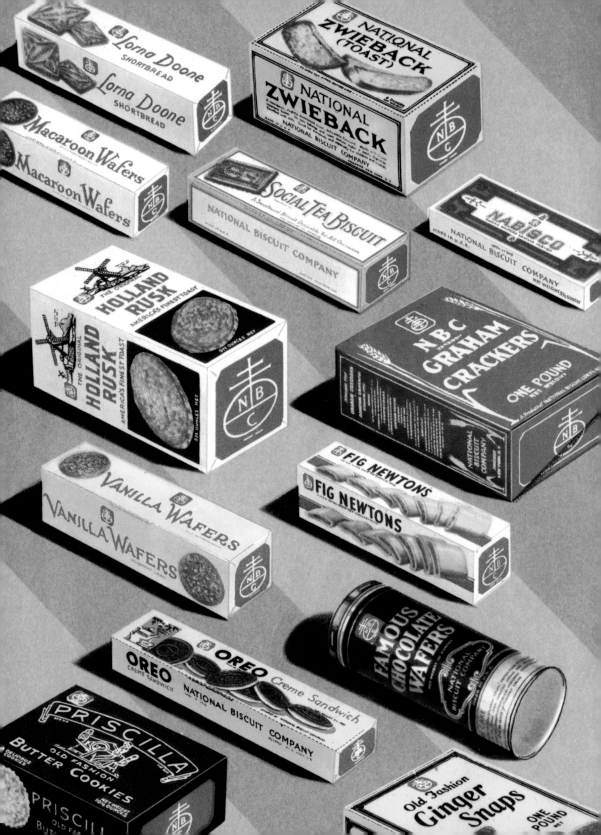

Pumpkin Chiffon Pie

INGREDIENTS

1 recipe crumb crust (page 10-11)

FILLING

1 cup canned pumpkin
3 egg yolks, slightly beaten
½ cup sugar
1 cup milk
½ teaspoon salt
½ teaspoon ginger
¼ teaspoon nutmeg
1 teaspoon cinnamon
2 tablespoons melted butter
1 tablespoon plain gelatin
¼ cup cold water
3 egg whites, stiffly beaten
½ cup sugar

Pies

DIRECTIONS

Place pumpkin in double boiler. Mix egg yolks, sugar and milk. Add to pumpkin with salt and spices and melted butter. Stir and cook until of custard consistency. Remove from heat, add gelatin which has been softened in cold water to hot pumpkin mixture and stir until dissolved. Chill, when mixture begins to stiffen, fold in slightly beaten egg whites to which has been added ½ cup sugar. Pour into baked crust. Sprinkle remaining crumbs over top. Chill in refrigerator 3 hours. May be topped with whipped cream before serving.

If the bananas you buy in the store have green tips like this... or are all yellow like this... let them ripen at home like this... ...at comfortable room temperature until they have brown flecks like this...

STOP Do not place bananas in refrigerator, as low temperatures prevent proper ripening.

Banana Chocolate Cream Pie

INGREDIENTS

½ recipe pie crust baked blind
   or
1 recipe crumb crust (page 10-11
2 squares (2 ounces)
   unsweetened chocolate
2 cups milk
¾ cup sugar
5 tablespoons flour
½ teaspoon salt
2 egg yolks, slightly beaten
1 tablespoon butter
½ teaspoon vanilla
3 ripe bananas, sliced
1 recipe whipped cream (page 11)
   (optional)

DIRECTIONS

Melt chocolate and milk in top of double boiler over simmering water, stirring until completely melted and well blended. Mix sugar, flour and salt and stir into chocolate mixture. Cook 15 minutes longer, stirring frequently. Whisk egg yolks in a small bowl and gradually add 3-4 tablespoons of the hot chocolate mixture to warm it and keep the eggs from curdling, then put the eggs mixture into the chocolate, stir and cook 1 more minute. Remove from heat and add butter and vanilla, stir and cool.

Cover bottom of prepared pie shell with ½ of the filling. Set aside 15-20 slices of banana and cover the filling with the remainder. Top bananas with second ½ of filling and then decorate with a circle of bananas around the perimeter of the pie. Serve with whipped cream if desired.

Chiquita Banana's Recipe Book, 1950

SUIT THE *Color* TO THE *Use*

TIPPED WITH GREEN?

The banana is partially ripe. The pulp is firm, starchy, slightly tart. Just ready to bake or broil or fry —cooking brings out a different, delicious flavor.

ALL YELLOW?

Now it's ready to eat or cook and use as an ingredient in baking.

FLECKED WITH BROWN?

Now it's fully ripe, at its best for eating, infant feeding and as an ingredient in baking. It's sweet, mellow, thoroughly digestible and delicious in fruit cups, salads, desserts and milk shakes.

Banana Whipped Cream Pie

INGREDIENTS

½ recipe pie crust baked blind
  or
1 recipe crumb crust (page 10-11)
Dash of salt
1 cup heavy cream
2 tablespoons sugar
Few drops vanilla
  or almond flavoring
4 to 5 ripe bananas
Toasted coconut

DIRECTIONS

Add salt to cream and beat until stiff enough to hold its shape. Fold in sugar and vanilla or almond flavoring. Cover bottom of pie shell with small amount of whipped cream. Peel bananas and slice into pie shell. Cover immediately with remaining whipped cream. Garnish with toasted coconut.

Important: Finely chopped nuts, grated semi-sweet chocolate or finely chopped, candied fruit peel may be used in place of the toasted coconut.

Chiquita Banana's Recipe Book, 1950

Banana Cream Pie

INGREDIENTS

½ recipe pie crust baked blind
  or
1 recipe crumb crust (page 10-11)
½ cup sugar
5 tablespoons flour
¼ teaspoon salt
2 cups milk
2 egg yolks, slightly beaten
1 tablespoon butter or margarine
½ teaspoon vanilla
3 ripe bananas

DIRECTIONS

Combine sugar, flour and salt in top of a double boiler. Add milk slowly, mixing thoroughly. Cook over rapidly boiling water until well thickened, stirring constantly. Cook 10 minutes longer, stirring occasionally. Stir small amount of mixture into egg yolks; pour back in remaining hot mixture while beating vigorously. Cook 1 minute longer. Remove from heat; add butter or margarine and vanilla. Cool.

Peel and slice bananas into pie shell; cover immediately with the cooled filling. Top with sweetened whipped cream, banana slices and other fruit, if desired; Or top with meringue made with 3 egg whites and 6 tablespoons sugar.

Coconut Cream Pie

INGREDIENTS

½ recipe pie crust baked blind
   or
1 recipe crumb crust (page 10-11)
⅔ cup sugar
½ cup flour
¼ teaspoon salt
3 egg yolks
2 cups milk
1 teaspoon vanilla
1 cup heavy cream
Toasted, shredded coconut

DIRECTIONS

Mix sugar, flour, and salt. Beat egg yolks; add milk. Stir into flour mixture, blending well. Cook over hot water until thickened, stirring constantly. Cover; cook 10 minutes. Cool slightly; add vanilla. Pour into baked pie shell; cool. Just before serving, whip cream until stiff and sweeten. Spread on pie. Sprinkle toasted coconut generously over cream.

Pies Men Like, 1953

Mrs. Evans' Kentucky Macaroon pie

INGREDIENTS

½ recipe pie crust (page 10)
½ cup sugar
pinch salt
3 egg yolks
2 cups milk
1 cup crushed macaroons
1 recipe meringue (page 11)
  made with 3 egg whites,
  6 tablespoons of sugar and
  ½ teaspoon almond extract
¼ cup chopped or slivered
  blanched almonds

DIRECTIONS

Preheat oven to 350°

Blend sugar, cornstarch, salt and eggs yolks together in top of a double boiler. Cook over simmering water until it is as thick as cream. Cool and add crushed macaroons. Pour into pie shell and bake at 325° or until firm. Turn oven down to 300°. Cover with meringue, sprinkle with almonds and bake at 300° until meringue is golden brown.

Pecan Pie

INGREDIENTS

½ recipe pie crust (page 10)
½ cup butter or margarine
1 cup sugar
3 eggs slightly beaten
¾ cup dark corn syrup
¼ teaspoon salt
1 teaspoon vanilla
1½ cups chopped pecans
Whole pecan meats

DIRECTIONS

Preheat oven to 375°

Chill pie shell thoroughly. Cream shortening. Add sugar gradually and continue beating until light and fluffy. Add eggs, syrup, salt, vanilla and chopped nuts. Pour into pie shell. Bake 40 to 45 minutes. Garnish with whole nuts. Serve with whipped cream if desired.

NEW! Chocolate Fudge Pie

MAGIC CHOCOLATE PIE

Here's the perfect pie for your next party. Extra-rich, fudgy chocolate pie topped with whipped cream. M-m-m . . . wonderful! (Makes one 8" pie.)

1 8-inch baked pastry shell, cooled
1⅓ cups (15-oz. can) Eagle Brand Sweetened Condensed Milk
2 ounces (2 squares) unsweetened chocolate

¼ teaspoon salt
½ cup hot water
½ teaspoon vanilla
½ cup heavy cream, whipped

1. Pour Eagle Brand Sweetened Condensed Milk into top of double boiler. Add chocolate and salt. **2.** Cook over rapidly boiling water, stirring constantly, until mixture thickens and drops, rather than runs from spoon, about 4 to 8 minutes. **3.** Stir in water gradually, keeping mixture smooth. Continue cooking, stirring occasionally, until mixture again thickens slightly, about 1 to 3 minutes.*

*__*4.__ Remove from heat. Stir in vanilla. Pour into pastry shell. **5.** Cool at room temperature for about ½ hour; then chill in refrigerator for at least 3 hours. Top with ½ cup heavy cream, whipped.

If glassware double boiler is used, cover and cook for 3 to 5 minutes until mixture thickens slightly.

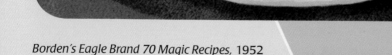

Cherry Cream Pie

INGREDIENTS

½ recipe pie crust baked blind
  or
1 recipe crumb crust (page 10-11)
2 tablespoons butter, melted
½ cup sugar
¼ cup cornstarch
½ teaspoon salt
1 cup milk
2 egg yolks
2 teaspoons vanilla
2 cups pitted cherries
  (or 16 oz. Can)
1 recipe meringue (page 11)

DIRECTIONS

Preheat oven to 300°

Combine melted butter, sugar, cornstarch, salt and milk. Cook over boiling water for 20 minutes, stirring frequently. Whisk egg yolks in small bowl. Pour small amount of milk mixture over egg yolks, stirring vigorously, then return egg yolks to milk mixture. Cook 2 minutes longer, remove from heat and whisk in vanilla. Cool. Put prepared cherries (drained if canned) in the bottom of the prepared pie shell, cover with cool custard, then cover with meringue. Bake for 15 minutes or until meringue is lightly browned.

Tempting, Thrifty, Wartime Meals, 1943

Ice Cream Pie

DIRECTIONS

Ice cream pie is a party pie. Try these fun filled variations in a pastry shell or a crumb crust, baked blind (see pages 10-11).

ICE CREAM PIE VARIATIONS

Peppermint Ice Cream Pie

Fill baked and cooled pie shell with slightly softened peppermint ice cream. Wrap in foil and freeze. Just before serving top with puffs of sweetened whipped cream and sprinkle with crushed peppermint.

Strawberry Ice Cream Pie

Fill baked and cooled pie shell with slightly softened strawberry ice cream. Wrap in foil and freeze. Just before serving cover with halved fresh strawberries and top with whipped cream.

Chocolate Sundae Ice Cream Pie

Fill baked and cooled pie shell with slightly softened chocolate chip ice cream. Wrap in foil and freeze. Just before serving top with whipped cream and shaved chocolate.

Pineapple Coconut Ice Cream Pie

Fill baked and cooled pie shell with slightly softened coconut ice cream. Wrap in foil and freeze. Just before serving cover with crushed pineapple and top with whipped cream.

Mint Meringue Ice Cream Pie

INGREDIENTS

1 crumb crust
 (page 11) baked blind
1 quart chocolate chip
 mint ice cream
3 egg whites
½ cup sugar

DIRECTIONS

Preheat oven to 500°

Pack ice cream into vanilla crumb crust (recipe on page 11) place in freezer for 1 hour, until very frozen. Beat egg whites until very foamy. Slowly add and beat in the sugar; beat until whites form stiff shiny peaks. Top pie with meringue. Be sure to cover ice cream completely, pressing meringue against crust to seal. Bake in a very hot oven, 500°, for 2 to 3 minutes. Serve at once.

PINEAPPLE

STRAWBERRY

LEMON

CHERRY

GOOSEBERRY

PEACH

Cakes and Pastries, 1923

Tarts

Tart cases are made from puff paste. Small patty tins are lined with puff paste and filled with dried beans. After they come from the oven the beans are removed to make room for the filling. The beans will prevent the paste from shrinking during the baking, the cases are then filled with the desired filling and brushed over with a good gloss. Most any kind of filling can be used for tarts but it should have a bright color and be of good quality.

Pecan Tarts

INGREDIENTS

1 recipe pie crust (page 10)
½ cup water
1 cup brown sugar
2 tablespoons flour
⅛ teaspoon salt
2 eggs
1 cup milk
½ cup whole pecan meats
1 teaspoon vanilla
½ cup cream, whipped with
  1 tablespoon powdered sugar

DIRECTIONS

Preheat oven to 450°

Line 10 small tart tins or muffin tins with pastry and bake blind (see page 10-11). Prepare medium thick syrup by boiling sugar and water together. Set aside to cool. Add flour and salt to lightly beaten eggs. Stir in the milk and mix well. Cook this mixture in double boiler until thick and smooth, stirring constantly. While hot add half of the brown sugar mixture. Stir in vanilla. Put one large tablespoon of mixture in each tart shell and place four pecans on top. Use the remaining syrup to cover the pecans. Put a teaspoon of sweetened whipped cream in the center of each tart. Chill thoroughly and serve.

Apricot Custard Tarts

INGREDIENTS

1 recipe pie crust (page 10)
¼ cup sugar
1 tablespoon cornstarch
⅛ teaspoon salt
1 cup milk, scalded
2 egg yolks
¼ teaspoon vanilla
1 recipe meringue (page 11)

APRICOT MERINGUE

½ cup dried apricots
3 tablespoons sugar
½ teaspoon lemon juice
2 egg whites

DIRECTIONS

Preheat oven to 450°

Line 10 small tart tins or muffin tins with pastry and bake blind (see page 10-11). Sift sugar, cornstarch, and salt together. Add hot milk, stirring constantly. Cook until slightly thickened. Add beaten yolks. Cook one minute longer. Add vanilla. Cool partially before pouring into baked pastry tart shells, then cover with apricot meringue.

Apricot Meringue

Soak dried apricots in cold water. Boil until very soft. Drain. Put apricots through strainer or mash thoroughly. Stir in sugar and lemon juice. Beat egg whites until stiff. Add apricot mixture and continue beating until the meringue holds its shape. Pile on top of custard. Do not bake.

Cherry Tartlets

INGREDIENTS

½ cup canned cherries, drained
3 tablespoons ground rice
  or rice flour
2 egg whites
4 tablespoons butter
  or margarine
¾ cup sponge cake crumbs
4 tablespoons sugar
2 tablespoons candied
  orange peel
½ teaspoon lemon extract
Pinch salt
1 tablespoon cream

DIRECTIONS

Cream shortening and sugar together, add ground rice, crumbs, peel, currants, cream, salt, lemon extract, and whites of eggs well beaten. Roll out pastry (recipe page 6), cut into rounds, line greased tartlet tins with rounds, put in each a tablespoonful of mixture. Bake in a moderate oven for 12 to 15 minutes. Top with cream if desired, and serve.

The Story of Crisco, 1913

Chocolate Orange Tarts

INGREDIENTS

1 recipe pie crust (page 10),
2 ounces Hershey's Baking
  chocolate, melted
1⅓ cups condensed milk
½ cup orange juice
Grated rind of ½ orange
2 oranges diced or cut in sections

DIRECTIONS

Preheat oven to 450°

Line 8 small tart tins or muffin tins with pastry and bake blind (see page 10-11). Melt chocolate in double boiler. Add condensed milk. Cook over hot water 5 minutes or until thick, stirring constantly. Beat smooth. Add orange juice and rind and beat thoroughly. Arrange diced or sliced oranges in bottom of pastry shells. Cover with chocolate mixture. Garnish with spoon of whipped cream and maraschino cherry, whole nut-meat, or bits of candied pineapple or ginger. Chill. Serve an assortment on fancy platter.

Chocolate Tartlets

INGREDIENTS

1 recipe pie crust (page 10)
3 squares unsweetened chocolate
  cut in pieces
2 cups cold milk
1½ cups sugar
4 tablespoons cornstarch
¼ teaspoon salt
2 egg yolks well beaten
½ cups seedless raisins
½ cup nut-meats chopped
1 tablespoon butter
1 teaspoon vanilla

DIRECTIONS

Preheat oven to 450°

Line 8 small tart tins or muffin tins with pastry and bake blind (see page 10-11). Add chocolate to milk in double boiler and heat. When chocolate is melted, beat with rotary egg beater until blended. Sift sugar, cornstarch, and salt together, and add to chocolate mixture; cook until thickened, stirring constantly. Cook 5 minutes longer, stirring occasionally. Pour small amount of mixture over egg yolks, stirring vigorously. Return to double boiler and stir until mixture thickens again. Remove from fire, add raisins, nuts, butter, and vanilla. Pour into tart shells. Cool. Cover with whipped cream.

Baker's Best Chocolate Recipes, 1932

7-Up Pie Crust

INGREDIENTS

1 cup sifted flour
½ teaspoon salt
¼ – ⅓ cup shortening
3 tablespoons chilled 7-Up

There's a place in your kitchen...for 7up

PANCAKE MIX
ALSO FOR WAFFLES

DIRECTIONS

Preheat oven to 425°

Measure flour and salt into bowl. Cut in shortening with a pastry blender or fork until particles are size of small peas. Add 7-up gradually, a few drops at a time, tossing with a fork to distribute evenly. Press into ball; allow to rest 15 minutes. Roll out on a lightly floured surface into a circle ⅛" thick. Fit into a 9" pie plate. Trim ½" from edge of pie plate. Fold this under and flute. Prick pastry with a fork. Bake about 15 minutes. Cool and fill.

You're Really Cooking, 1957

DIRECTIONS

Mix 1 tablespoon of Hawaiian Punch Base with apples, rhubarb, peaches or berries.

Hawaiian Punch Recipes, 1950s

Index

7-Up Pie Crust 70
Apple Pie + variations 13
Apple Pie 14
Apricot Custard Tarts 65
Banana Chocolate Cream Pie 51
Banana Cream Pie 54
Banana Pie 17

Banana Whipped Cream Pie 53
Blueberry Pie 31
Brown Sugar Meringue 11
Butterscotch Pie 38
Butterscotch, Coronation Pie 43
Caramel Pecan Cream Pie 46
Cherry Cream Pie 59

Cherry Pie (canned) 34
Cherry Pie (fresh) 29
Cherry Pie + variations 35
Cherry Tartlets 67

Chocolate Coconut Cream Pie 47
Chocolate Cream Pie 36
Chocolate Fudge Pie 58
Chocolate Orange Tarts 68

Chocolate Sundae Pie 44
Chocolate Tartlets 69
Chocolate, Angel Pie Dessert 37
Coconut Cream Pie 39
Coconut Cream Pie 55
Cranberry Meringue Pie 23
Cream Pie, Standard 45

Crumb Pie Shell 10
Custard Pie 41
Graham Cracker Cream Pie 46
(Grape) Aunt Jane's Vintage Pie 19
Hawaiian Fruit Pie 71
Ice Cream Pie, Variations 60
Jelly Pie 15

Lemon Pie 22
Lemon, Marvel Pie 24
Macaroon,
  Mrs. Evans Kentucky Pie 56
Meringue 11
Mint Meringue Ice Cream Pie 61
Molasses Crumb Pie 42
Nut Pie Shell 10
Orange Blossom Pie 25
Peach, Golden Lace Pie 26
Pecan Pie 57
Pecan Tarts 64
Plain Pastry 10
Puff Pastry 10
Pumpkin Chiffon Pie 49

Pumpkin Pie 27
Pumpkin, Bettina's Basic Pie 21
Rhubarb Pie 33
Strawberry Custard Pie 32
Strawberry Pie 18
Streusel 11
Whipped Cream 11

Cover	*Home Baking Made Easy*, 1953
Endpapers	*For Making Good Things to Eat*, 1930
Frontispiece	*Electric Range Recipe and Canning Book*, 1950s
Copyright	*Rawleigh's Good Health Guide*, 1952
Title page	*Rawleigh's Good Health Guide*, 1952
Page 48	*50 Delicious Desserts*, 1930s
Page 63	*New Recipes for Good Eating*, 1948
Page 72	*Praise for the Cook*, 1959
Page 73	Advertisement, 1948